MW01609886

My Name is Nina!

English Conversations for Kids

Natalia Bochorishvili
Vitalij Palkus

My Name is Nina!

English Conversations for Kids

Natalia Bochorishvili
Vitalij Palkus

Addison-Wesley Publishing Company

A publication of the World Language Division

Editorial Development: Karen Howse
Layout and Production: Karen Howse
Cover Photograph: Zane Williams
Additional illustrations: Andrej Kouleshov and Iskra Kouleshova
Manufacturing: James W. Gibbons

ISBN: 0-201-83263-1
1 2 3 4 5 6 7 8 9 10-CRS-00 99 98 97 96

Contents

UNIT 1. What's your name?

Student Book pages 4-5

KEY EXPERIENCES

- Getting acquainted
- Introducing friends

KEY LANGUAGE

- What's your/his/her name?
- My/his/her name is ...?
- Hi, I'm ...
- This is my friend, ...
- Nice to meet you.
- Where are you from?
- Where's he/she from?
- I'm/he's/she's from ...
- Pronouns: I/my, you/your, he/his, she/her, we/our, they/their
- Verb: to be
- family members

SUGGESTED ACTIVITIES

1. Play the tape for the first two conversations as students follow along in their books. Discuss the pictures at the top of page 4 (Nina, Jerry, Maria).
2. Have students work in small groups asking each other's names and introducing each other.
3. Play the tape for the bottom of page 4 as students follow along in the book. Discuss the characters speaking. Explain that *mom* and *dad* are informal words for *mother* and *father*. Ask students to suggest names for them. Ask questions such as: *Where are they from? Where's Taro from? Where's Nina/Jerry/Maria from?*
4. Play the tape for page 5 as students follow along in their books. Discuss names and countries. Have students work in pairs to create conversations between the characters.
5. Ask students to tell about their friends/classmates. Write any new names and countries on the board.
6. Reproduce the blackline master on page 7 of this guide for each student. Circulate around the class, helping students complete the page if necessary.

Write about these children.

_____   _____
_____   _____
_____   _____
_____   _____

Draw a picture of yourself. Write about yourself.

_____

_____

_____

_____

_____

_____

_____

_____

_____

_____

UNIT 2. Hi! How are you?

Student Book pages 6-7

KEY EXPERIENCES

• Greeting people formally and informally

KEY LANGUAGE

• Hi, hello
• Good morning, good afternoon, good evening
• How are you?
• I'm fine/Fine, thanks/ Just fine/Very well/Not very well, I have a cold
• morning, afternoon, evening, night
• sun, bird, bee
• cat/kitten, dog/puppy

SUGGESTED ACTIVITIES

1. Introduce and explain times of the day. Practice the pronunciation of *morning, afternoon, evening*. Ask students, *Is it morning/afternoon/evening/night now?* Have them look at the picture on page 6 and ask the same questions.
2. Introduce *sun* and *bird* using the picture on page 6.
3. Play the tape once as students follow along in their books. Play the tape again, having students repeat each exchange. Then have students role-play the conversation between the three friends.
4. Explain that *hi/hello* are informal greetings, and *good morning/good afternoon/good evening* are formal. Note that in modern usage *good morning/afternoon/evening* mean *hello*, and *good night* means *good-bye*. Also explain *fine, thanks* is informal while *fine, thank you* is formal. Then have students walk around the classroom greeting each other both formally and informally.
5. Discuss the picture on page 7. Introduce new words.
6. Have students work in pairs or in groups of three to make conversations between the bees on page 7. Give them two conditions: 1) the bees do not know each other and the conversations should start with introductions, then rather formal greetings, or 2) they are old friends.
7. Play the tape for page 7 and have students repeat the conversation. Ask students to tell the names of their pets and to show how they greet them when they get home.
8. Reproduce the blackline master on page 9 of this guide for each student. Circulate around the class, helping students complete the page if necessary.
9. Play the tape for the songs on pages 8 and 9 of the student book. Have students listen to the songs and sing along. Return to these songs as often as possible—just for fun.

Write conversations between these children.

_____   _____

_____   _____

_____   _____

_____   _____

Write your conversation with Nina.

Hi, Nina. _____?

_____ and you?

_____

9

UNIT 3. How old are you?

Student Book pages 10-11

KEY EXPERIENCES

- Talking about age
- Learning numbers one to one hundred

KEY LANGUAGE

- How old are you/they?
- How old is he/she/your sister?
- I'm .../you're .../they're .../he's .../she's .../Mary's ...
- Numbers: one through one hundred
- Family members: mother/mom, father/dad, sister, brother, grandmother, grandfather

SUGGESTED ACTIVITIES

1. Practice counting. Have students count from one to twenty, looking at the numbers in the box on page 10. Then write some numbers on the board and ask students to say the number.
2. Explain how to count on from twenty: twenty one, etc. to one hundred. Have students look at the numbers at the bottom of page 11. Write more numbers on the board (from twenty to one hundred) and have students say the number,
3. Introduce the question *How old are you?* Ask students to tell their age.
4. Play the tape for page 10 and ask, *How old is the boy? How old is the girl?* Have students work in small groups asking each other, *How old is your sister/brother/best friend/mother/father,* etc.
5. Show photographs of people of different ages and practice *he/she's nearly ... He/she's about ...*
6. Play the tape for page 11 and have students fill in the blanks, encouraging them to give different answers. Ask, *And what do you think?* Have them start their replies with *I think he/she's ...*
7. Reproduce the blackline master on page 11 for each student. Circulate around the class, helping students complete the page if necessary.

Complete a conversation between the girls.

How _____?

I think, _____.

And I _____ about.

_____.

Oh, no!

Put the numbers on the clock. Write the numbers on the lines first.

one _____   _____

_____   _____

_____   _____

_____   _____

_____   _____

UNIT 4. What is it?

Student Book pages 12-13

KEY EXPERIENCES

• Asking about and naming objects

KEY LANGUAGE

• What is it?
• What's in there?
• Is it a (dog)? Yes, it is./No, it isn't.
• Imperative: Open it!
• Plurals: car/cars, toy/toys

SUGGESTED ACTIVITIES

1. Play the tape for page 12 as students follow along in their books. Then discuss the picture with the class, talking about the gifts and pointing out the objects. Introduce new words, *Christmas tree, balloon, car, truck, boat, train, camera, teddy bear, walkman, sneakers.*
2. Show students how to form plurals: balloons, cars, etc. Ask students to continue.
3. Point to various objects on the page. Ask, *Is it a (train)?* Then switch the question, *What is it?* pointing to the same object.
4. Have students work in pairs: one thinks of an object in the classroom, and the other tries to guess the object, *Is it a (clock)?*
5. Play the tape for page 13 as students follow along in their books, repeating the conversation.
6. Play a new game. Put classroom objects into a paper bag. Let students take turns feeling the bag but not looking inside. Have them guess the object. *Is it a pencil?*
7. Reproduce the blackline master on page 13 of this guide for each student. Circulate around the class, helping students complete the page if necessary.

Name the objects.

b_____   d_____

c_____   c_____

t_____   r_____

Now color the objects and cut them out.

UNIT 5. There's one man.

KEY EXPERIENCES

- Identifying people/animals
- Counting

KEY LANGUAGE

- There's only one ...
- There are many ...
- Irregular plurals: man-men, woman-women, child-children, tooth-teeth, foot-feet, goose-geese, mouse-mice, ox-oxen, sheep-sheep, deer-deer

SUGGESTED ACTIVITIES

1. Play the tape for page 14 and ask students to repeat all of the nouns they hear both in singular and plural.
2. Have students read the lines in turn. You start the sentence, *There is ...* Have a student continue by saying *one man*, then another students continues with *one woman.*
3. Ask students to count men, children, feet, etc. in the picture at the bottom of page 14. Explain that *lots* means *many.*
4. Play the tape for page 15 and ask students to describe the animal farm. Ask, *Are there many cows?/horses*, etc. *Is there one mouse?* Draw attention to regular vs. irregular forms of plural in the nanes of the animals. Give more words for animals in the picture, *a horse, a cow, a pig, a sheep, a goose, a hen, a chick, a mouse.*
5. Reproduce the blackline master on page 15 for each student. Circulate around the class, helping students complete the page if necessary.

Write the words for the pictures.

	One	Many
	woman	_women_
	_____	_____
	_____	_____
	_____	_____
	_____	_____
	_____	_____
	_____	_____

15

UNIT 6. How many? How much?

Student Book pages 16-17

KEY EXPERIENCES

• Identifying food/drink

KEY LANGUAGE

• Many (with countable nouns)
   many drinks/bottles
   many pizzas/sandwiches/hamburgers
   many dollars
• Much (with uncountable nouns)
   much water/juice/milk
   much food/sugar/salt
   much money
• fast food, pizza, hamburger, meat, fish, vegetables, salad
• soft drinks, sodas, juice
• head, neck, shoulders, arms, fingers, legs, knees, feet, toes, hair, face, ears, eyes, nose

SUGGESTED ACTIVITIES

1. Play the tape for page 16 as students follow along in their books. Ask, *Where is this taking place? How many children are there? How many pizzas/drinks, etc. did they order?*
2. Explain that *How much is it?* means *How much does it cost?*
3. Explain that *many* is used with countable nouns, and *much* with uncountable nouns. Give examples.
4. Have students work in small groups, role-playing the scene. Then have them practice ordering food and asking for costs.
5. Bring food and clothing advertisements from catalogs or magazines to class. Have students work in pairs, practicing, *How much is it?*
6. Play the tape for page 17 as students follow along in their books. Introduce the vocabulary at the bottom of the page, having students repeat after you.
7. Play the song again, modeling the actions by pointing to each body part as it is sung. Play the song again, and have students sing along and do the actions.
8. Reproduce the blackline master on page 17 for each student. Circulate around the class, helping students complete the page if necessary.

Nina wants to buy some fruits. Write her conversation with the clerk.

How much are the _____?

_____. And how _____ do you want?

_____.

And some _____, please.

How _____?

_____.

Now count the fruits like this.

_____ *There are five pears.* _____   _____

_____   _____

_____   _____

_____

UNIT 7. What's your favorite color?

Student Book pages 18-19

KEY EXPERIENCES

- Identifying/describing clothes
- Learning colors

KEY LANGUAGE

- What's your favorite color?
- I like ...
- hat, jacket, pants, sweater, skirt, shirt, T-shirt, dress, shorts, coat, suit, swimsuit, shoes, boots
- yellow, red, pink, purple, green, blue, brown, gray, black, white
- Personal and possessive pronouns: I-my, you-your, he-his, she-her, we-our, they-their

SUGGESTED ACTIVITIES

1. Discuss the picture on page 18. *Nina and Maria are in a store.* Introduce words for clothes and colors. Ask, *What are Nina's favorite colors? How about Maria?* Have students describe Nina's and Maria's clothes.
2. Play the tape for page 18 as students follow along in their books. Explain the phrase, *Isn't it cute?* and give some similar expressions, *Isn't it nice? Isn't it pretty?*
3. Have students role play the conversation.
4. Have students work in pairs, describing each other's clothes.
5. Play the tape for page 19 and have students identify the clothing using color words from the box at the bottom of the page.
6. Reproduce the blackline master on page 19 for each student. Circulate around the class, helping students complete the page if necessary.

Draw clothes on the children. Then color the pictures.

Write about the children.

Beth	**Jean-Paul**
Her favorite colors are	His favorite colors are

Her _____

her _____

and her_____

UNIT 8. I'm big, I'm small.

Student Book pages 20-21

KEY EXPERIENCES

• Describing objects/people/animals

KEY LANGUAGE

• big, small, short, tall, long, weak, strong, thin, fat, happy, sad
• elephant, mouse, donkey, giraffe, worm, snake, lamb, wolf, monkey, cat, girl

SUGGESTED ACTIVITIES

1. Introduce new words, *It's an elephant, It's a big elephant,* etc. Explain the use of articles *a/an* and compare *a mouse* (before words beginning with consonants) and *an elephant* (before words beginning with vowels).
2. Play the tape for page 20 as students follow along in their books. Ask students, *What is the elephant saying?* etc.
3. Explain opposites, *short man/tall man,* etc. Practice opposites pointing to various objects and people.
4. Describe yourself, *I'm tall, strong,* etc.
5. Have students work in pairs, giving true or false statements and reacting to them. For example, *I'm old. No, you're not, you're young.*
6. Play the tape for page 21 and have students complete the activity, writing the opposites on a separate piece of paper. Then ask them to compare the results with a partner.
7. Reproduce the blackline master on page 21 for each student. Recite each line of the poems and have students repeat after you.

Repeat after your teacher. Then read the poems yourself.

There was an Old Man with a nose,
Who said, "If you choose to suppose
That my nose is too long, you are certainly wrong!"
That remarkable Man with a nose.

There was an Old Man who said, "Hush!
I perceive a young bird in this bush!"
When they said, "Is it small?" he replied, "Not at all!
It is four times as big as the bush!"

UNIT 9. Her eyes are blue. ────────────

Student Book pages 22-23

KEY EXPERIENCES

• Describing people

KEY LANGUAGE

• His/her hair is blond. He/she has blond hair.
• His/her eyes are blue. He/she has blue eyes.
• have/has
• blond, red, black, fair, dark

SUGGESTED ACTIVITIES

1. Ask students to describe the girl and two boys in the top picture on page 22. Then play the tape, stopping after each line for students to repeat.
2. Play the tape for the bottom of the page as students follow along in their books. Ask students, *How would he describe his sister?*
3. Have students describe their brothers/sisters/mothers/fathers, using vocabulary from this and previous units.
4. Play a guessing game. Divide the class into two groups, each group describes someone from the other group, and the second group must guess who is being described.
5. Give out pictures and photographs of some famous people. Ask students to describe them.
6. Play the tape for page 23, and have students describe the people using words from the bottom of the page. Then have students describe each other.
7. Reproduce the blackline master on page 23 for each student. Circulate around the class, helping students complete the page if necessary.

Connect the dots. Color the pictures.

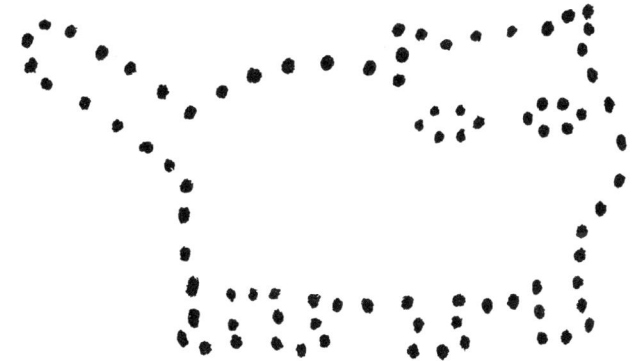

Describe and compare the pictures.

A fat _____   A big _____
Color _____   Color _____
Tail _____   Tail _____
Eyes _____   Eyes _____

UNIT 10. Where is it? ————————————

Student Book pages 24-25

KEY EXPERIENCES

• Describing objects
• Describing locations

KEY LANGUAGE

• Where is it?
• It's on/in/under/between/behind
• house, walls, roof, door, room, window, table, chair
• tree, river, bridge

SUGGESTED ACTIVITIES

1. Play the tape for page 24, and have students describe where the mouse is using the prepositions at the top of the page.
2. Play the hiding game. Hide some objects (pens, books, etc.) in the classroom and ask students where they are.
3. Ask students about the positions of various objects in the room, *Where is my desk? Where is the door?*
4. Have students describe their rooms at home.
5. Play the tape for page 25, and discuss the picture with the class. Introduce new words. Have students complete the sentences.
6. Reproduce the blackline master on page 25 for each student. Circulate around the class, helping students complete the page if necessary.

Look at the picture. Answer the questions.

1. Where is the bank? _____

2. Where is the post office? _____

3. Where is the bridge? _____

4. Where is the park? _____

5. Where is the horse? _____

6. Where is the car? _____

UNIT 11. I'm sorry.

Student Book pages 26-27

KEY EXPERIENCES

• Giving and accepting apologies

KEY LANGUAGE

• Excuse me.
• I'm sorry.
• That's all right.
• No problem.
• Can you hear me?
• Sorry, I can't hear what you're saying.

SUGGESTED ACTIVITIES

1. Read and discuss the conversations on page 26. Comment on the uses of *excuse me* in the sense *I'm sorry* (as in this unit) and also to attract someone's attention, *Excuse me, what's your name?* Give variants of how to say you are sorry, *Oh, I'm sorry. I'm so sorry. I'm terribly sorry.* Introduce possible polite replies, *That's all right, That's OK. No problem.*
2. Play the tape for page 26. Draw attention to the intonation.
3. Have students role-play situations where they have to apologize and reply to apologies.
4. Ask students to repeat the telephone conversation at the bottom of the page. Working in pairs, have them make up a similar conversation where they cannot hear each other and keep apologizing. Encourage students to keep the conversation going as long as possible.
5. Have one of the students speak for the little monkey on page 27, and distribute the roles of other animals among other students. Ask students, *What are they saying, What are they thinking?*
6. Reproduce the blackline master on page 27 for each student. Circulate around the class, helping students complete the page if necessary. Then have students role-play their conversations.

Write a conversation between the boy who dropped the cup and the old woman.

_____   _____

_____   _____

_____   _____

_____   _____

_____   _____

UNIT 12. What time is it?

Student Book pages 28-29

KEY EXPERIENCES

• Asking for/telling time

KEY LANGUAGE

• What time is it? (inversion)
• Do you know what time it is? (direct word order)
• It's (five o'clock)./It's (five).
• It's half past/quarter past/quarter to (five).
• Sorry, I don't know.
• clock, watch, a.m., p.m.

SUGGESTED ACTIVITIES

1. Describe how to tell time in different ways: *one o'clock, half past one* or *one thirty*, etc. Say and write the time in all different ways, including, *It's 12:00, It's twelve o'clock, It's noon, It's midnight.* Explain abbreviations *a.m.* and *p.m.*
2. Play the tape for page 28 pausing after each phrase for students to repeat.
3. Have students work in pairs asking and telling time.
4. Go around the class asking students questions, *When do you get up? When do you leave for school?* etc.
5. Play the tape for page 29, and have students work in pairs to complete the activity. Suggest some models, *What do you do at 8 o'clock in the morning? I brush my teeth*, etc.
6. Reproduce the blackline master on page 29 for each student. Circulate around the class, helping students complete the page if necessary.
7. Play the tape for the songs on pages 30 and 31 of the student book. Have students listen to the song and sing along. Return to these songs as often as possible, just for fun.

Write the time in all possible ways.

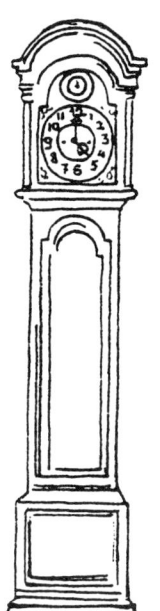

_____

_____

_____

_____

_____

_____

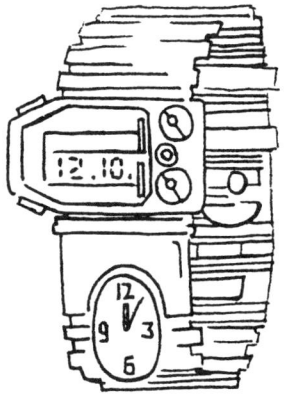

_____

_____

_____

_____

_____

_____

29

UNIT 13. Yes, please. No, thanks.

Student Book pages 32-33

KEY EXPERIENCES

• Using polite requests and responses

KEY LANGUAGE

• Do you want ...
• Yes, please./No, thanks.
• How about ...
• Here you are.
• Thank you.
• cookie, orange

SUGGESTED ACTIVITIES

1. Play the tape for page 32 as students follow along in their books. Then ask students, *Does the girl want a cookie? How do you know? What did she say? How about an orange?*
2. Go around the class asking students, *Do you want an apple/an orange/a piece of candy*, etc.
3. Have students role-play the conversation on page 32.
4. Collect a few objects at the front of the class. Ask each student, *Can I have a (pencil) please?* and have the student pass it to you. Model response, *Here you are.* Then have students work in pairs doing the same activity. Model polite responses, *Thank you./Thanks. You're welcome.*
5. Play the tape for page 33, and have students work in pairs to complete the activity.
6. Reproduce the blackline master on page 31 for each student. Have students work in small groups. Circulate around the class, helping groups complete the page if necessary.

Draw a picture of yourself and your friends around the table.
Write a conversation. Start with *Do you want ...*

UNIT 14. Do you speak English?

Student Book pages 34-35

KEY EXPERIENCES

• Discussing languages and nationalities

KEY LANGUAGE

• Do you speak (English)?
• Does he/she/Nina/Jerry speak (English)?
• Yes, he/she does. No, he/she doesn't.
• English, Spanish, French, Russian, Italian, German, Japanese, Chinese
• He/she speaks (English).

SUGGESTED ACTIVITIES

1. Play the tape for page 34 as students follow along in their books. Ask, *Does Nina speak English? What languages does she speak? Does Maria speak Spanish?* etc.
2. Have students role-play the conversation between Nina, Maria and Jerry.
3. Play a game. Have students work in pairs asking each other, *Do you speak (Spanish)*, repeating the question with other languages. The student who names the most languages wins.
4. Play the tape for the passages on page 35. Have students work in pairs to make conversations between the characters.
5. You can extend the activity by using the picture on page 5 of the student book. Introduce the pattern: Country-Nationality-Language, *Nina is from Russia. She is Russian. She speaks Russian.*
6. Reproduce the blackline master on page 33 for each student. Circulate around the class, helping students to complete the page if necessary.

Write about each of these children.
Where is he/she from?
What languages does he/she speak?

_____

_____

_____

_____

_____

_____

_____

_____

UNIT 15. Can you swim?

Student Book pages 36-37

KEY EXPERIENCES

• Describing abilities

KEY LANGUAGE

• Can you swim?
• Sure.
• I can't swim at all.
• can/can't (cannot)
• sing, dance, cook, swim, ride a horse, ride a bike, ski, skate, play tennis/basketball/football/hockey, play the piano/violin/guitar

SUGGESTED ACTIVITIES

1. Play the tape for page 36 as students follow along in their books. Then have students role-play the conversations in pairs.
2. Have students ask you questions starting with Can you ... Introduce various answers, Sure. No problem. *I can (swim) very well. I can (play tennis) but not very well. I can't ...*, etc.
3. Have students work in pairs asking each other about various abilities. Introduce vocabulary from KEY LANGUAGE above.
4. Ask students to report on what they learned about their classmates' abilities using the pattern *He/she can (sing), but he/she can't (dance).*
5. Play the tape for page 37 as students follow along in their books. Ask, *Can Nina dance? Can she cook?* etc. Then have students describe what they can and cannot do.
6. Reproduce the blackline master on page 35 for each student. Circulate around the class, helping students to complete the page if necessary.

Write about what these children can do.
Also write which of these things you can do.
Then write which of these things you can't do.

35

UNIT 16. She dances very well.

Student Book pages 38-39

KEY EXPERIENCES

• Describing likes and dislikes

KEY LANGUAGE

• She dances very well./She likes to dance./She loves to dance.
• What do you do after school?
• What do you like to do?
• Simple present tense

SUGGESTED ACTIVITIES

1. Explain the difference between *I can swim* (ability to swim) and *I swim* (do it regularly). Go around the classroom asking students various *Can you ...* and *Do you ...* questions.
2. Play the tape for page 38 as students follow along in their books. Ask questions about the characters, *Does Nina dance? Where does she dance? Does she like to dance? How about Sen-Lin?*
3. Have students work in pairs making a conversation between Nina and Sen-Lin.
4. Ask students what they do after school. What do they like to do. Help with unfamiliar words to describe various activities and sports.
5. Play the tape for page 39 and have students complete the exercises. Then compare your students likes and dislikes with those of the children in the book.
6. Reproduce the blackline master on page 37 for each student. Circulate around the class, helping students to complete the page if necessary. Then collect the pictures and play a guessing game: *Who plays the piano? Who plays football,* etc.

Look at the pictures. Write what you can and cannot do.
Then write what you like to do and what you do not like to do.

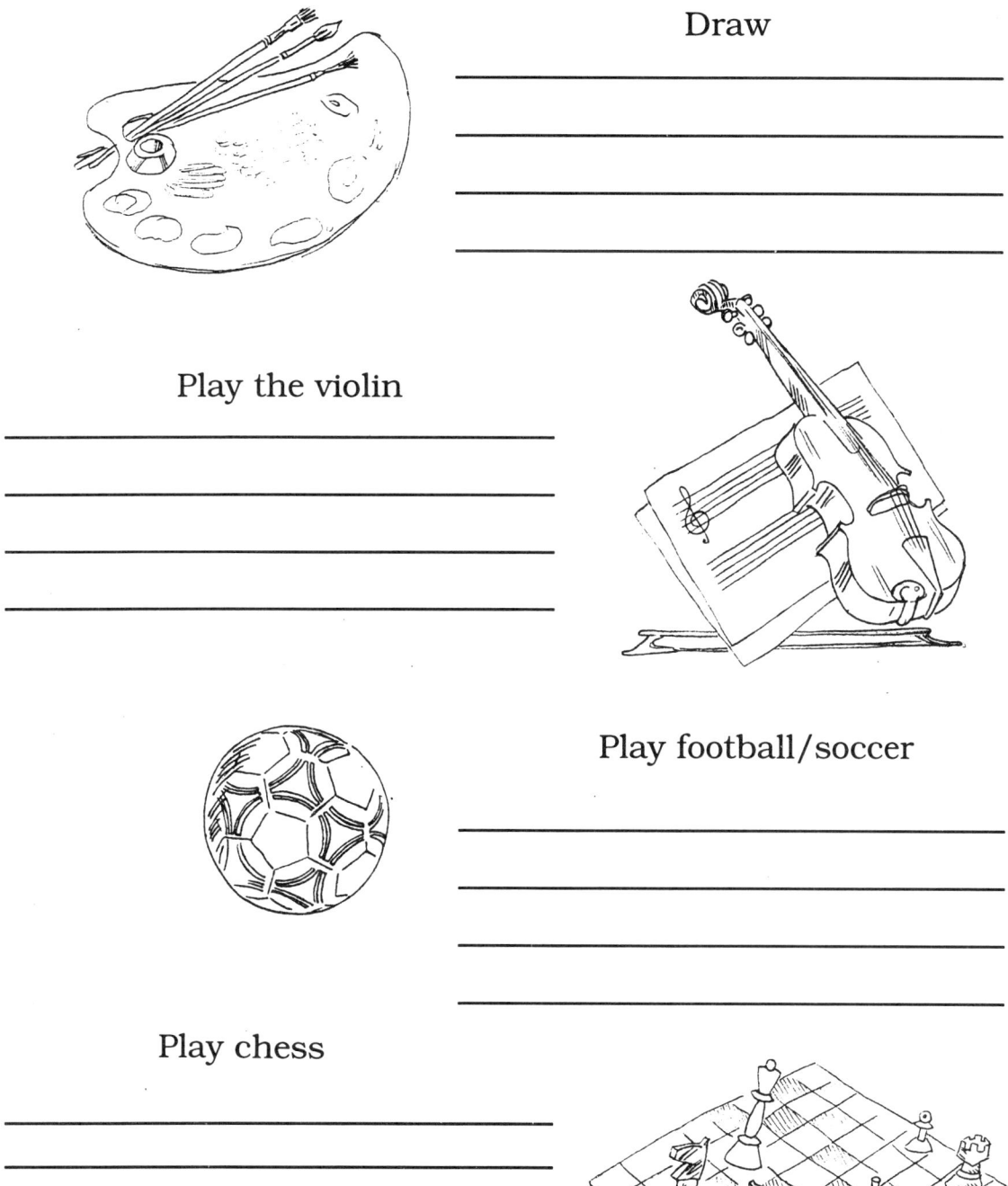

Draw

_____

_____

_____

_____

Play the violin

_____

_____

_____

_____

Play football/soccer

_____

_____

_____

_____

Play chess

_____

_____

_____

_____

_____

UNIT 17. Come in. Go away!

Student book pages 40-41

KEY EXPERIENCES

• Giving orders, commands, and instructions

KEY LANGUAGE

• Phrasal verbs: Come in, Come here, Get out, Go away, Take away, Stop, Sit down, Stand up, Keep quiet, Listen, please

SUGGESTED ACTIVITIES

1. Play the tape for page 40 as students follow along in their books. Have students repeat the commands.
2. Have students work in pairs, giving each other orders and instructions. For example, *Stand up. Turn around.*, etc. Introduce more phrasal verbs to help them avoid repetition.
3. Practice phrasal verbs with opposite meanings, *come in/go away, bring/take away*, etc.
4. Together with students, read some instructions and/or recipes and draw their attention to the use of imperatives.
5. Play the tape for page 41. Then have students complete the page. Encourage them to use imperatives besides those suggested in the activity.
6. Reproduce the blackline master on page 39 for each student. Circulate around the class, helping students to complete the page if necessary. Then have students role-play the teacher's commands.

What is the teacher saying to the students?
Write five sentences using imperatives.

_____   _____

_____   _____

_____

UNIT 18. Don't worry.

Student book pages 42-43

KEY EXPERIENCES

• Expressing concern

KEY LANGUAGE

• Come on!
• Don't say that.
• Don't worry.
• Don't cry.
• Don't tell.
• Don't push me.

SUGGESTED ACTIVITIES

1. Discuss the picture on page 42. Ask students to guess what is going on and what the conversation is about.
2. Play the tape for page 42 as students follow along in their books. Stop after *Come on, Dad* and explain the meaning of *come on.*
3. Ask three students to role-play the conversation.
4. Pretend that you are leaving the room. Give instructions, *Don't stand up. Don't open the door. Don't go out,* etc.
5. Play the tape for page 43 and have students work in pairs to complete the activity. Discuss situations when these phrases can be used.
6. Reproduce the blackline master on page 41 for each student. Circulate around the class, helping students to complete the page if necessary.

Nina is worried. She may be late for her tennis class.
What is her mother saying to her?
Write five sentences, three of which start with *Don't...*

_____

_____

_____

_____

_____

UNIT 19. Whose is it?

Student book pages 44-45

KEY EXPERIENCES

• Expressing ownership

KEY LANGUAGE

• Possessive pronouns: my-mine, your-yours, his-his, her-hers, our-ours, their-theirs
• Possessive 's: Mary's, Nick's
• Possessive s': parents', students'
• apartment, music, violin, sports, tennis racket, take pictures, camera, pen, pencil, ruler, brush, watercolors, hammer

SUGGESTED ACTIVITIES

1. Play the tape for page 44 as students follow along in their books. Have students role-play the conversation.
2. Explain the use of possessive pronouns. *Is this your umbrella?* (with a noun) and *Is this yours?* (without a noun.) Then explain possessives: *Betty's, Nick's* (possessive 's) and *parents'* (possessive s').
3. Practice possessives using pictures from previous units. Ask questions with *Whose...*
4. Have students work in small groups, asking who various objects belong to, *Is this your bag? Is this Tom's pen? Whose book is it?*, etc.
5. Play the tape for page 45, introducing any unfamiliar words. Have two students read the page out loud. Then have them continue to play the roles of Polly and Peter, agreeing or disagreeing when other students discuss who the things in the picture belong to. For example, Student: *It's Polly's camera.* Polly: *Yes, it's mine.* Peter: *Yes, it's hers.*
6. Reproduce the blackline master on page 43 for each student. Circulate around the class, helping students to complete the page if necessary.

Nina, Maria, and Jerry see some things that they lost in the Lost and Found.
Write a conversation between them.
Start with *Is this ...*

LOST AND FOUND

_____

_____

_____

_____

_____

_____

UNIT 20. See you later.

Student Book pages 46-47

KEY EXPERIENCES

• Saying good-bye

KEY LANGUAGE

• Good-bye, bye, see you later, see you (tomorrow/next week/on Thursday)

SUGGESTED ACTIVITIES

1. Play the tape for pages 46-47 as students follow along in their books. Have students repeat the phrases.
2. Introduce more parting phrases and explain their meaning: *Good-bye* (general), *bye* (informal), *good night* (before going to bed), *have a nice day* (when parting in the morning), *See you later* (when parting for a short time), *See you later, alligator* (used jokingly among children), *Take care* (used instead of good-bye).
3. Have students work in pairs making up short conversations and ending them with various parting phrases.
4. Have students role-play Nina and her friends' conversation. Encourage them to use all possible ways to say good-bye.
5. Reproduce the blackline master on page 45 for each student. Circulate around the class, helping students to complete the page if necessary.
6. Play the tape for the song on page 48 of the student book. Have students listen to the song and sing along.

Snow White is saying a good-bye phrase to each of the dwarfs.
Each is a different phrase.
Write what she is saying.

_____

_____

_____

_____

_____

_____

45